Wealth is a Mind$et 2nd Edition by SHYNNA MITCHELL

Wealth is a Mind$et 2nd Edition by SHYNNA MITCHELL

Wealth is a Mind$et

2nd Edition

Written By:

SHYNNAMITCHELL

● ● ● ● ● ● ● ●

Wealth is a Mind$et 2nd Edition by SHYNNA MITCHELL

CONTENTS

Acknowledgments

I thank God for giving me the courage, vision, strength, and energy to write the 2nd edition of my book.

Husband, Symon Mitchell for encouraging me to finish my book & add some personal stories so that my book can be more relatable. Also, for helping me balance everything while doing so.

Children Antalise, Shylise, Destiny, Shiloh, and Eric. I do this for you all. I know you all witnessed my work of passion. So, therefore, I know it somehow rubbed off on you all. One day you all will go for your passion as well.

Mother, Helen Ridgeway McCown, and Father, the late Larry McCown, R.I.P. who always encouraged me to be my own boss. Who also told me... "Yes, go for it!" when it came to supporting all my business ideas.

Brother, Larry McCown for always sharing powerful knowledge and inspiring me. Special thanks for collaborating with me and spreading financial literacy by facilitating, Wealth is a Mind$et workshop for the T.R.U.E program inside a Connecticut prison, where I previously facilitated a tailor-made speaking engagement.

My late Aunt, Glenda Ridgeway, R.I.P. was the first one to advise me about credit at an incredibly young age. She always told me to "pay your bills before the due dates to establish & maintain A-1 credit".

To the number of wonderful people that booked me for speaking engagements, interviews, and workshops. Real Estate clients, and customers that purchased the 1st edition of this book that asked, "when are you going to write another book"? I say to you all...thank you! That time has come!

Much Gratitude!

Peace, Love & Happiness

-Shynna Mitchell

Maiden Name: McCown

EMPOWERING YOU TO BUILD YOUR EMPIRE...

The Financial Fanatic PRESENTS
Wealth is a Mind$et 2nd Edition

By: SHYNNA MITCHELL shares a collection of relatable financial awareness topics along with strategies & motivation to encourage you to 'think big' when it comes to getting big results while building your empire.

"Mind renewing financial ideas to help you to cultivate financial growth."

—SHYNNA MITCHELL _____

To book SHYNNA MITCHELL for consulting services, speaking engagements, seminars/events contact the Author at Email: info@wealthisamindset.org

S H Y N N A M I T C H E L L . . . .

Providing Financial & Business Empowerment Techniques

"Knowledge empowerment to help you build and maintain a fruitful life."

SHYNNA MITCHELL The Financial Fanatic Financial & Business
Empowerment Coach/Author /Speaker/Realtor

I wrote, Wealth is a Mind$et 2nd Edition 5 years later during the COVID-19 Pandemic, with additional knowledge and experiences since the 1st Edition in sincere hopes that I may be able to inspire others to do as I have done—take control of your money and your livelihood. As a realist, I knew that in order to see progress it had to begin with a mindset shift. So, I took the time to explore various ideas, practices, and concepts to create a system that would work together to help me become more fruitful— just as I pray that you will do the same. Reaching success in all areas of your life (mentally, physically, financially, and spiritually) depend upon key factors such as:

1. Your willingness to sacrifice.

2. Your ability to take on new challenges.

3. How you react, prepare and adapt to life's uncertainties,

and finally;

4. Your dedication to the realization of your goals.

5. Your realization, "that every action has a reaction".

If you are ready for your new lane of the journey toward a 'lifetime change' Wealth is a Mind$et 2nd Edition offers key life strategies and wealth-building principles to help you as you seek to build and maintain your empire. Get ready to get in your new lane!

Email: SHYNNA MITCHELL at
Wealthisamindset.org

Shynna Mitchell
The Financial Fanatic

"Empowering You to Catch the Wealth Mind$et Vibes."

–SHYNNA MITCHELL

Education, Empowerment, Choices, and Changes help you to build and maintain a healthy Mind$et of Wealth...

Wealth is a Mind$et 2nd Edition

Is all about education, empowerment, choices, change, a vibe, a new lane, and action!

Are you ready to explore your new lane, your new vibe, and take charge of your life? If so, having a pure-wellness wealth blueprint system designed to help you construct your personal success model may be exactly what you need to take your dreams and level up. When you decide to take charge of your life you will begin to embrace change by establishing goals (financial goals, educational goals, health goals, relationship goals, and maybe some new like-minded friends, etc.) that will ultimately shape you and inspire you to reposition yourself for your ideal success, because everyone has a different definition of success. Be sure to respect one's differences, God purposely made each one of us different. Look at things from a different lens sometimes. One of my favorite slogans is "different strokes for different folks".

Success at any level requires vision, proper planning, training, and being accountable... all of which are a series of actions that will ultimately bring about a result— [a New Mindset].

It is important to understand a true sense of a wealthy mindset. Wealth is more than just something that you own, possess, or what you can show in your bank account. It is an overall wellness position of who you are, your mind, body, spiritually, and financially. In life, you must be well-rounded and stay even keel.

A mind is a terrible thing to waste. Have you ever bought an item that required assembly then tried putting it together without reading the instructions? I am sure many of us have. However, we all know that if we miss a screw or a latch the likelihood of that item withstanding wear & tear is slim. This also holds some truth for your wealth mindset model. If you miss key elements of your wealth blueprint, you can run the risk of compromising the longevity of your success or become complacent plus take you longer to get there. Better yet, if you don't have a blueprint, how would you know once you have reached a success level if you don't know where you're headed.

//Wealth in generational stages.

As a child, my parents basically, taught me what was instilled in them, which included discussions about the importance of creditworthiness and maintaining financial success. Therefore, I too, have passed these teaching along to my children. However, there are many children today that have lacked these teachings. The majority were taught to finish school and get a good job.

Generation-by-generation we are led by a lack of knowledge or other hindering situations that allow us to miss the opportunities to train our children for the financial part of their life's journey. Therefore, we must break the chains of financial bondage so that we broaden our horizons in all efforts to elevate our future.

Now times have changed. It is a new millennium where the struggle has made us hustle and many has bossed up and taken the lead of their money-making opportunities. This is the entrepreneur era.

I strongly believe that no matter where you are in your life or how big/small your goal sets are, implementing a wealth process can prove to bring rewarding results. In fact, by putting into motion your success plan of action you will begin to identify your strengths and weaknesses, recognize your pitfalls and begin to set your life in a new direction—ultimately feeling better about yourself; physically, mentally, emotionally financially, and spiritually.

<u>Challenge Yourself To Recondition Your Mindset With</u>

<u>The 3 C's</u>

Choices

Chances

Changes

Matter...

Recondition Your Mind$et

Why do choices, chances, and change matter?

"If you don't choose to take a chance you will never experience change."

-Ingrid N. Allen, Author

Give an example of choices that can be made in your life that you feel would enhance your overall success.

• Educational Choices

• Financial Choices

• Community Involvement Choices

• Marriage Choices

• Social Choices

• Relocation Choices

• Investment Choices

• Circle of Influence Choices aka (Your 5 Closest Friends)

_____

_____

_____

Give an example of chances that you may want to explore in your life that you feel would enhance your overall success.

• Pursuing your educational goals

• Seeking out a new financial opportunity (new job, starting a business, etc.)

• Investing in real estate

• Becoming involved with my community awareness program

• Getting married

• Meeting new friends

_____

_____

_____

Give an example of changes that you may want to make in your life that you feel would enhance your overall success.

• Do the right things for the right reasons

• Removing your limited belief (faith)

• Speaking things that you want into existence

• Changing your attitude & Staying Even Keel

• Being consistent with your goals

_____

_____

_____

CHAPTER

ONE

WEALTH IS A MIND$ET

● ● ● ● ● ● ● ● ●

CHAPTER ONE

WEALTH IS A MIND$ET

Understanding how to manage money and invest as a means to build financial security is a critical need in our communities. Most parents and grandparents living in the inner-city were not taught financial literacy during their upbringing. Rarely are their discussions concerning the importance of saving money. People in the urban areas are not given instructions on the purpose of money and how to utilize it when they get it. Therefore, the urban community members end up developing an impoverished mindset.

Wealth is not just a material reality; Wealth is a Mind$et. It begins with education about acquiring and managing money. Saving and investing are equally important. An impoverished mindset stems from a lack of financial knowledge. With constantly hearing the reverberations of "Living the American Dream" ("The Life") throughout their childhood and simultaneously feeling like an outcast to the rest of society. When combined with a sense of hopelessness in ever obtaining such a material life for themselves, some of these urban community members begin to value the look of material wealth and seek to attain it by any means necessary. Financial Literacy workshops will teach financial security via saving, budgeting, investing, home and business ownership benefits individuals and the community as a whole.

When members of a community are financially educated and secure, the crime rate can be significantly reduced, and the community at large would be safer. For years and to this day my brother, Larry facilitates Wealth is a Mind$et workshop for the T.R.U.E program in a Connecticut Prison for emerging adults, ages ranging from 18-25.

It should also be understood that financial illiteracy does not only exist within urban communities. Career Builder reported that 8 in 10 U.S. workers live paycheck to paycheck. The Federal Reserve Board discovered that 44% of American households surveyed could not cover a $400 emergency expense. So, if people who are making a decent salary are living this way, we must teach members of our communities that a Job merely means "Just Over Broke" if they are not financially educated.

Empowerment Techniques to Recondition Your Mindset:

▪ *Seek a financial literacy workshop for you and your family. (Children Included).*

▪ *Go Back to School if need to for higher education and a higher-paid profession.*

▪ *Challenge yourself to cut out buying unnecessary material items. Remember the old saying "if it's not broke, don't fix it". So don't go buy a new iPhone every year when they come out.*

NOTES:

Knowledge is Priceless & Powerful.

Education is an Asset.

Recondition Your Mindset & Secure the Bag.

✓ *Identify the Bag*

✓ *Get the Bag*

✓ *Secure the Bag*

✓ *Repeat.*

Secure The Bag

CHAPTER

TWO

THE RICH STAY RICH & THE POOR STAY POOR

● ● ● ● ● ● ● ● ●

CHAPTER TWO

THE RICH STAY RICH V& THE POOR STAY POOR

The wealth that is passed down from generation to generation is called generational wealth. The inheritance of money, businesses, homes, vehicles, land, assets, and investments are all examples of generational wealth. Fortunately, some are born into wealth, which is a blessing! When people are born into wealth they are taught differently. From birth, they were taught what to do and how to carry on with their financial status. Therefore, they have different vibes, views, and values about life and money. However, if the rich do not do as they were taught as it relates to their finances, they can and will eventually go broke. They must make a conscious decision to continue their wealthy legacy and keep the bag up. Sidenote: Try mimicking the rich, not the Joneses.

Unlike the rich, some were not "born with a silver spoon in their mouth's" which

society classifies as middle-class or poor.
Yet, that does not mean that they must be or
stay a product of their environment. The
poor/middle-class must have the desire to
want a different financial status. Therefore,
they must become disciplined and strive for
success towards financial freedom. In Curtis
Jackson's [aka 50 Cent] voice "Get Rich or
Die Trying." In my words "Don't be no
slouch or a lame!" I am not saying to greed
for money. I am saying make a difference
for your generation and get your bag up.
You must do certain things and create habits
for you to secure the bag so it can stay up,
"If It's Up, Then It's Up, Then It's Up, Then
It's Stuck" in Cardi B's voice, lol!!

The 21/90 rule states that it **takes 21
days to make a habit and 90 days to make
it a permanent lifestyle change.** The
easiest way to break a habit is to replace it
with a new one.

As a child, my family was considered
'the high-end middle-class'. Some back
then, considered as "rich" or referred to us

as the Huxtables from the hit 80's/90's TV
Show called The Cosby Show.

My dad, Larry McCown (who has
transitioned), worked at Pratt & Whitney
airplane plant for many years as a Welder.
My mom, Helen Ridgeway McCown
worked for several departments for the City
of New Haven and is an entrepreneur. Both
of their jobs were considered great jobs.
However, my father wanted and felt that he
needed more to be able to live the lifestyle
that he had desired. He always enjoyed
driving foreign cars. He also dressed on the
high-end, designer scale, like

Super Fly, literally, no cap, lol! Only if you
could see my father's pictures from back in
the day, you would be like, right! But most
of all, my dad knew that he wanted to be his
own boss. So, he set his sights on becoming
a nightclub owner. Once he bossed up with
his plan and acted on it, he successfully
opened his first nightclub—Larry's Lounge
in New Haven, CT, plus managed the Osias
Night Club at the same time then years later

he opened a 2nd nightclub, LL's Lounge in
Rochester, NY.

When he brought the nightclub,
his strategic plan also included two
apartment units just above, which he
planned to rent for additional income. This
wealth-building tactic is considered multiple
streams of income as well as passive
income. The rental properties were
considered passive income because he made
money off them in his sleep. My dad did not
need to lift a finger to generate that money.

The passive income also afforded our
family the financial freedom to take
vacations and other luxuries without my
father overworking himself. This is what I
believe sparked my interest in Real Estate. I
can remember as a child, I would watch my
parents manage and sometimes even help
them with minor touch-ups or repairs for the
rental turnover.

My dad was a smart businessman; he
had an accountant that came over every
Saturday to go over 'the books'. Being the

wise man that he was, he would also have his children around to watch how things worked—being your own boss. All-in-all I can honestly say he instilled great entrepreneurship qualities and lessons within us as we are a part of The New Millennium.

He gave my brother Larry the D.J position, which was known as at the time, DJ Shawnie B., during happy hour because he was the oldest. He also gave my little sister, Shyneka, and me little odd jobs on the weekend to help with putting up the delivery items such as the candy bars and stuff. Of course, I always got my Snicker bar out of the deal every time! Those were my favorite!

Overall, my dad did many things just to teach us about running our own business. That is how I became such a serial entrepreneur today! Friends often would ask me..." How do I do it"? Generally, my response is... "I Just Do It", "but understand, that everyone was not built to be an entrepreneur." "I was raised by business-minded parents." So, I guess it is true as the old saying goes... "An apple doesn't fall too far from the tree" in other words teach your children because they are watching and learning from you. Leaders create repeaters.

//Pass on your knowledge about wealth... // Put others up on game... It is enough out here in this world for those that are determined to eat, to eat.

Once you have realized your vision of wealth and have educated yourself on the road to getting there, in this 'sink or swim' generation, you must pass down your wealth of knowledge to help educate others. When I say help others, I do not mean give them handouts, that would only cripple them. I mean, if they ask for help or didn't ask for your help and that is your friend or family member, but you see them putting in the work and they just need some advisory. Otherwise, we continue the risk of creating generation after generation of individuals who are barely making it or living check-to-check.

I can go on and on, but I am more than certain you have heard all of this before. Why not take heed, catch these vibes and switch lanes? However, you must admit if you keep hearing the same old sayings repeatedly, they must apply to you or maybe some truth to it in some way, form, or fashion.

//Take accountability and be wise...

Be wise and take responsibility for your financial education, your spending & wealth planning decisions. Now, you cannot blame your parents for you being brought into this world without a 'silver spoon' because they cannot help what they did not know. Debt, work hard, love, and family bonds may be the only thing that was passed down to them. Therefore, I am so passionate about encouraging you to make a change within your current generation. In other words, do not live beyond means.

//Consciously consider the difference between the look of material wealth and true financial freedom...

I often hear individuals make fun of what someone is wearing; if it is the latest style or if someone's shoes are 'busted'. In most cases, I can almost guarantee that the person that is being talked about has money in the bank and assets. Generally, a person that seeks to have financial freedom is more interested or concerned about their banking and saving accounts, versus how they look. So,

sacrificing that high-priced designer handbag or over-priced shoes is not a big deal.

I must admit that I am a little guilty of wanting and getting some of those designer items. My husband spoils me, and we have balled out from time to time. However, we do not go overboard and do not put those wants before our priorities. Besides some of those designer shoes hurt my feet, surprisingly, considering how expensive that they are. I am just about over it, maybe just certain shoes. The price we pay to stay in tune with the latest fashion.

On the flip side, often I'll think business-minded. I do know those expensive designer items are also assets and can be sold for profit at any given time if there is ever a need. Example: A plain Rolex without diamonds do not easily lose their value over time. See, being a Millionaire does not = $1 Million in your bank account, it can be a mixture of things, you can be a Millionaire on paper such as the result of the large total market value of the assets you own.

In this text, I wrote some quite common sayings in a rudimentary fashion, so that the words cannot be misinterpreted. In other words, some things you do not know can hinder your financial growth.

Though you may be rich at heart and mind, I encourage all who read this book to consciously consider the difference between the look of material wealth vs. the realness of the bag for financial growth. To make necessary sacrifices and do not focus on what you can lose, focus on what you can gain by catching the vibes to get your bag up and for it to stay up. Remember, having a lack of knowledge about finances will leave you blind and broke forever.

Empowerment Techniques to Recondition Your Mindset:

- *Stay in your lane. Everything is not for everybody & that it is ok.*

- *Stop making the luxury designers and foreign car manufacturers rich, they are already wealthy. Find ways to build wealth for your family.*

- *Manage your checking/savings accounts daily/weekly. Do not be afraid to look at it.*

- *Mimic the wealthy, not the Joneses.*

- *Successful people leave clues, so follow great influencers. Always remember you can choose to resist, but we can also choose to learn from influencers and appreciate that they too have a place in the kaleidoscope of life.*

N OTES:

Knowledge is Priceless & Powerful.

Education is an Asset.

Recondition Your Mindset & Secure the Bag.

✓ *Identify the Bag*

✓ *Get the Bag*

✓ *Secure the Bag*

✓ *Repeat.*

Secure The Bag

CHAPTER THREE

COVID 19- The Wake-UP Call

● ● ● ● ● ● ● ● ●

CHAPTER THREE

COVID 19- THE WAKE-UP CALL

What is it going to take for you to wake up and address your financial status; a tragedy, job loss, and unable to collect unemployment? Let the wake-up call be now, while you are reading this book!

REWIND, Scratch that, the above was a paragraph from the 1st edition of Wealth is a Mind$et that was published in 2015, just 4 years before COVID-19. Only if you the readers of that the 1st edition had taken heed to the game I was providing then, they would have been 10 steps ahead and had their Wealth Mind$et already reconditioned.

Now, look what tragedy just took place in 2019 and is still ongoing till this day in 2021. The COVID 19 Pandemic. It got real. If the words Corona, COVID 19, Pandemic did not wake you up, I dislike being the one who says it, but there is little hope for you and the only way now is to pray to God and put in the work. You know the saying, "Prayer and Without Work is Dead".

//Sit back, catch the vibes, take heed to the game I am providing, take notes, boss up, get in your new lane and make moves...

"Sit back, catch the vibes, take heed to the game I am providing, take notes, boss up, get in your new lane and make moves to be successful in securing the bag to build and maintain your empire"! I know, I just said a whole lot, so hopefully, you caught something out of it. No more saying things in a soft, well-mannered tone, I want these words to stick.

With that all being said, I have a confession to make: In the past and when I first made my day view with presenting the 1st edition of this book, I was still living under the impression of growing up in the '80s, yes I'm an 80's baby, but when being diverse was not publicized, being unapologetically black was not as of receptive yet nor did we have a voice. Yes, we went through the Black Panthers Movement and a few others but yeah it was not like it is today. We have come a long way, yes, but we still have a way to go. I must say thanks to social media and all the new technology that has been a help for Blacks to let their voices be heard.

Now back to the point: If you do not know where you are going, how will you know when you get there? When an engineer creates a huge sky loft building do you think they will start the job without a blueprint? Absolutely, not! So, why would you decide to build your empire without goals? —which, brings me to the topic of goal setting. Overall, your wealth depends on your ability to set and carry out your goals. There are many different types of goals that are generally self-defined. Therefore, it's up to you to figure out which areas are most important for you to direct your focus. As a rule of thumb when I start my goal-setting regimen I begin with my short-term goals—which once accomplished, ultimately help me to gain the confidence to set and achieve my long-term goals.

As we set our personal and financial goals, we must be mindful of taking a realistic approach. Oftentimes, we tend to set goals that require long-term planning expecting to accomplish them in only a short time. This can ultimately set us up for failure and may affect how we go about our future goal-setting roadmap.

Now, do not get me wrong, I am not saying to limit your goal objectives. But more so, just to be aware of the time, resources, and network that it will take to reach your desired results.

Small realistic goals may be things that you would like to accomplish within five years or less. While long-term goals may take longer and give you something to look forward to. Short-term goals help to empower you and give you a sense of self-gratification and the confidence that you need to stay on target. Your short-term goals should be daily, weekly monthly and should bring you closer to your long-term goals. In the end, your life should reflect the goals that you have chosen to pursue. Helping you to maximize your potential and satisfy your positive instincts.

Whether you have set a goal to buy a car, go to college, start investing, buy a home or start a business you must think about the sacrifices that you will need to make in order to make that goal become a tangible reality.

Visualization helps you to see your plan for healthy wealth building.

Generally, in every successful situation, there must be a vision of what success looks like. So, first, we must examine ourselves to find out what inner materials we already have and what elements are necessary to construct 'our' success framework.

Your wealth blueprint should highlight various angles, parallel references, and tactics that will guide you in the direction of change. Of course, designing your wealth blueprint will take time. However, the planning period will prove to be "time well spent" in the long run.

Make a vision board—also known as a dream board. Vision boards were created for you to get excited about your life visions! Do you remember when you were in 1st grade and creating seemed to be fun? Well, revisit that time in your life by reenacting those emotions. Act like a big kid; have fun and enjoy cutting out things you want to manifest in your life. Think about what you really would like to do. Then just go for it! Place your vision board at home where you can see it all the time. Also, make a mini one so that you can place it at your job if permissible or business!

Once I have written down a clear statement of my goal(s) and have created my vision board it is then that I take the necessary steps toward accomplishment. Consequently, committing myself to a successful conclusion.

Journalizing your journey.

While going through my financial trials & errors and overcoming obstacles within my journey, I found my journal to be one of the most effective tools in helping me to keep my goal initiatives in perspective.

It's funny, but as I decided to write the 1st edition of this book, I was thumbing through some of my old journal notes and ran across some of my documented goals. Of course, I am in awe today here in twenty-twenty one [2021] living the reality of my dreams as a serial entrepreneur.

Throughout the journey, I can honestly admit that by writing and revisiting my journal notes I became more in-tune with my thought process, which has helped me to put together a more substantial plan to achieve my success.

Plan for the best and prepare for the worst.

When I worked in the mortgage industry with a Georgia program that helped homeowners save their homes, I read through so many sad letters on how people suddenly lost their job, became ill, or lost a spouse due to death or separation/divorce. Life at times catches you by surprise. Beat the surprises to the punch!

For each hardship letter that I read, I thanked God for my health, a roof over my head, my job, my family, and for the insight to think ahead. Create an emergency fund to be able to pay your bills for up to six months. Make sure you take advantage of short- and long-term disability if your job offers it. If not, purchase a plan outside your job. Build a relationship with your car insurance agent. Most big major car insurance companies sell different types of policies such as renters, homeowners, life just to name a few.

//Budgeting helps you to separate your needs vs. wants...

Budget your finances and reach higher. To properly budget your finances, you must first be 'real' with yourself as it relates to your income as well as your expenses. Successful budgeting also depends on your willingness to make

51

sacrifices. Though sacrifice is not always easy, it helps to give you a full view of those things that may cause your finances to flourish or suffer.

When someone makes a sacrifice, it is always for something else. Are you willing to now take the sacrifice to get to the next level that awaits you? Sit down as a family to establish your living necessities and your wants. Then make a conscious effort to sacrifice to watch your financial life grow. If you are single the same method applies.

Becoming financially stable before you enter a relationship helps you to plan your future and eliminates most financial strains or stress. You will then be able to focus on building a fantastic life together without having to worry about money.

Funny, but I had a friend who was committed to budgeting. For years, I watched her diligence in how she would spend her money. Most people thought she was just being cheap, all the while she was just smart about money and her future financial status. When we would go hang out sometimes on the weekend, she would carpool to save money on parking and rush to get to wherever we would go before the venue would start charging a fee. One of our mutual friends and I would gripe about it...combatively telling her that if we went too early place will be empty. We would be the ones to go late, be willing to pay the extra fee for the skip line, VIP style, just to make our grand entrance! That friend that was big on being frugal early on in life, I must say I am proud of how she conducted her financials since she moved out on her own in her early 20's and appears to still be doing good to this day.

//Think ten steps ahead...

Don't just think for the moment and forget about it. Always think ten steps ahead. Don't wait until you are down to your last dollar to use your head.

Also, don't ever spend your last dollar until your next one comes in. Meaning, do not count on expected money until you get it in your hand. Oftentimes when we are owed money or if someone says they are going to give us money we tend to count that promissory as 'actual income'—pretty much like we view a paycheck. However, for the most part, our paycheck is guaranteed (if we show up for work). This type of thinking causes us to overspend or leave us in debt. So be mindful of your actual income and get a grip on your spending before it is too late.

Plan your retirement. You hear it all the time that Social Security may not be available to you by the time you retire. Don't think it's just something they're saying just to say. Prepare yourself. There are enough warning signs. Take heed. Save a dollar today and you will be grateful for it tomorrow. It will add up and come in handy. You can't ever have too much money or planning strategies.

Your Employer 401k Plan

Taking full advantage of your employer-sponsored 401K Plan is a tool that will help you to accumulate income for your retirement or future investments, especially if your company offers dollar matching, that's free money. If you don't that's considered leaving money on the table. It is important to think about your retirement as Social Security Income or Disability Income may not be around forever. Many young individuals think that planning for retirement in their 20's is just crazy. But the truth is...the earlier you start the better your financial position will be when you reach retirement age.

For the Entrepreneurs, I didn't forget about you, you can open a Solo 401(k) plan that allows you to make far higher contributions to your retirement plan than if you are an employee in an employer 401(k). **Any self-employed person can open a solo 401(k) plan regardless of the**

55

product or service you provide.

For example, if you start investing $50.00 per paycheck or you may want to double or triple that amount if you are a business owner and do not get paid weekly or bi-weekly, you may get a big commission check, royalty payments, etc... Therefore, if you're an entrepreneur from the age of 25 until the age of 65 (depending on the interest rate), just imagine how much you may be able to accumulate. Now, don't get me wrong, this does not replace your budgeting plan. However, it can very well be a good 'nest egg' that you have access to if you should need it.

Some entrepreneurs that I have met capitalized on using a portion of their 401K funds as their business start-up capital versus going to the traditional funding institutions. However, keep in mind there may be early withdrawal tax penalties that may be accessed should you decide to use the money before you are eligible to retire. So, be sure to do your due diligence when it comes to comparing your options.

Budgeting overview

Write down a list of all your expenses, starting with the necessary items. Then create a list of all your income. Everything must be accounted for to be a realistic budget. So, it's best practice to make sure you list everything—including hair bundles, nails, lashes, makeup, treats, entertainment, and anything else that you may purchase or like to do regularly.

A person without a budget will always be broke because they lack proper management. Therefore, much of what they do often leads to chaos. Always remember, if you have a bag and you do not budget you will eventually become broke. Wealthy people always budget their finances or hire someone to do it for them, so they can keep account of what they have. Again, your budget must be realistic. If there are things that you know you can't live without, include those items within your budget. However, if there are things that you know you can sacrifice, do it to see results.

Let's try out a sample budget sheet:

SAMPLE BUDGET WORKSHEET

Income

Employment Salary (1) $_____ Employment Salary (2) $_____ Cash Surplus $_____ Child Support/Alimony $_____ Investment Income $_____ Other Income Resources $_____

Total Income $_____

Expenses

Rent/Mortgage $_____yr./mo.
Homeowners/Rental Insurance $_____ yr./mo.
Non-Employer Deducted Taxes $_____ yr./mo.
Household Items $_____ yr./mo. Utilities $_____ yr./mo. Internet/Cable/Telephone $_____ yr./mo. Transportation/Car Payment $_____ yr./mo. Parking $_____ yr./mo. Child Care $_____ yr./mo. Insurance (Car) $_____ yr./mo. Gas $_____ yr./mo. Insurance (Life/Disability/Medical) $_____ yr./mo. Groceries /Dining $_____ yr./mo. Clothing $_____ yr./mo. Laundry/Dry Cleaning $_____ yr./mo. Entertainment $_____ yr./mo. Travel (Business/Personal) $_____ yr./mo. Education/Training $_____ yr./mo. Gifts/Contributions $_____ yr./mo. Grooming (Hair/Nails) $_____ yr./mo. Savings/Retirement Plan $_____ yr./mo.

Total Expenses $_____

■

The Wealth Mindset Challenge

■

• Write down your goals.

• Next to each goal note whether the goal is Long-Term or Short-Term.

• Keep your goal-setting log in a visual place so that you will be able to review them daily.

• Check off your list of each goal that you have accomplished.

• Then take the necessary time to celebrate yourself for your accomplishments. (ex. Treat Yourself, Clap, Sing, Dance, etc.) This exercise will help to boost your self-esteem, give you gratification and help you to continuously work toward your ambitions.

My Short-Term Goals Are...

→

_____

_____

→

_____

_____

→

_____

_____

→

_____

_____

My Long-Term Goals Are...→

_____

_____

→

_____

_____

→

_____

_____

→

_____

_____

Empowerment Techniques to Recondition Your Mindset:

- *Be 'real' with yourself as it relates to your income, expenses and realistic with your goals.*

- *Surround yourself with positive, like-minded individuals that too have a mindset of wealth.*

- *Don't hesitate to say, "I don't have it to spend." Or just not right now.*

  (Don't be afraid to simply say "No." when comes to protecting your financial budget).

- *Properly assess your needs vs. wants.*

- *Make a vision board.*

NOTES:

Knowledge is Priceless & Powerful.

Education is an Asset.

Recondition Your Mindset & Secure the Bag.

✓ *Identify the Bag*

✓ *Get the Bag*

✓ *Secure the Bag*

✓ *Repeat.*

Secure The Bag

CHAPTER

FOUR

PAY YOURSELF FIRST

● ● ● ● ● ● ● ● ●

CHAPTER FOUR

PAY YOURSELF FIRST

Whoot, Whoot, TGIF [Thank God it's Friday] or another note [The Grind Includes Friday! Okay, so it's Friday! —Payday for most. But wait...take a moment to think before your make any actions! Pay yourself first. Then, figure out your bills to pay.

Bills will always be here, so if you continue to pay your bills first you will feel like you have no money left to pay yourself, invest and save. This mentality is generally referred to as a "poor state of mind". Even if you save $25 a week, it will add up. Something is better than nothing. Just watch how your money grows. If you don't be wise about your finances no one else will for you for sure.

If you are an entrepreneur, especially make sure to pay yourself first. For some odd reason, entrepreneurs think that they should pay themselves last. Entrepreneurs must be very disciple about their finances even more than if you clock in. You will be your own company's employee. Cut yourself a check when you cut your employees a check if you have some.

One of the things I would advise you to do also is to have the amount of money that you would like to save come out of your paycheck automatically each pay period to go directly into your savings account. Or you can transfer the money yourself from your checking to your savings account first thing payday before you pay anything or anybody.

I would recommend trying one of your local Credit Unions or small local Banks. They tend to have fewer fees and are more likely to lend to you.

Also, some Banks have awesome tools on their websites that will help you calculate your net worth. That's pretty dope—I think. You will not only be able to state your financial status but will also be able to state your net worth.

You work hard for your money. Don't

you think you are worth something too? Also, after a full work period treat yourself to something. You deserve it. Now I'm not saying splurge and buy a new TV, I mean something more like your favorite restaurant or something minor. Take a moment now to think how much you may be worth?

Your Net Worth

Net Worth Cash Flow

Assets $_____

            Income $_____

Liabilities $(_____)

            Expenses $(_____)

Net Worth $_____

            Surplus/Deficit ($_____)

Your net worth = assets - liabilities.

Therefore, it is important to evaluate your liability choices against your assets so that you can increase your financial worth.

Your cash flow = income - expenses.

Your cash flow situation has everything to do with your spending habits. As mentioned earlier in the text eliminating unnecessary or excess expenses can help you as you move closer to your achieving your goals. Living above your 'means' only keeps you in financial bondage.

Empowerment Techniques to Recondition Your Mindset:

▪ *Consider yourself a bill and pay yourself starting next pay period.*

▪ *Set up a checking and savings account if you don't already have one. Be sure to contact your Human Resources Department to set up a direct deposit.*

▪ *Entrepreneurs, contact a CPA (Certified Public Accountant) for more information on paying yourself and putting money aside to pay your taxes.*

NOTES:

Knowledge is Priceless & Powerful.

Education is an Asset.

Recondition Your Mindset & Secure the Bag.

✓ *Identify the Bag*

✓ *Get the Bag*

✓ *Secure the Bag*

✓ *Repeat.*

Secure The Bag

CHAPTER

FIVE

MULTIPLE STREAMS OF INCOME

● ● ● ● ● ● ● ● ●

CHAPTER FIVE

MULTIPLE STREAMS OF INCOME

How many streams of income do you currently have coming into your household? If it's only one, you should hurry to generate another form of income. There should be more than one income per adult, per household, at least two streams of income per adult.

Once you become an adult and gain responsibilities, you should always have multiple streams of income. A job is not a lifetime income. Consider your job temporary even if you are not a temporary employee and you have been on your job for 15 years because your position or you can be eliminated at any given point or time and without warning. Remember, the keyword, EMPLOYEE. You're not the boss. You can be fired or in the nice words your boss may use is, laid off.

Set yourself up with multiple resources of where your money will come from. Think of your passion and explore ways to monetize it. We all know that we must work for the most part. So, why not embrace something you would love to do and do it! Let's go! Take me for an example; I continue to work as a Realtor full-time while writing this book, building my husband and I, New Real Estate Brand, 2SLM Properties, as well as us investing in a fleet of vehicles to put on Turo, a car share platform.

Now, I didn't say it was easy and I had plenty of rough days and long nights. Some days I felt like it just wasn't enough time in a day. But I had to be wise and gain balance. The children played tug-a-war with my time. After all, we realized it was all worthwhile! Now I have another experience to share with the world!

Create a business doing what you love. Not go find a part-time job. A part - job, will have the same consequence there as well. Become your own Boss! Become a business owner. Therefore, you will always have control or know the warning signs of business slowing up and be able to make a different business move to keep that one income afloat.

One example for instance is, if you work overtime on your job, all those extra hours you worked you won't see all the extra money you were expecting because the more money you make the more you are taxed.

When you think of creating multiple streams of income, one income or more should be passive income. Passive income is money that will continue to make

while you are sleeping, without you physically working for it. You can be on vacation and that money will still come in. For example, owning an ATM. That machine works on its own. It does not require you to be present in order to make the money; you just collect the money.

Another example is a laundromat or a daycare. If you are the owner of these types of businesses, however, do not work daily within the business because you hire employees, that business will provide passive income for you. The money will still be made no matter if you are ill or no matter where you are at. I don't know about you, but that sounds fabulous to me!

Don't be in denial and deprive your opportunities. There is plenty of room in this world for everyone to do something different or even be in the same lane. Go out and make it happen!

To passive income!

2nd Edition by SHYNNA MITCHELL

Empowerment Techniques to Recondition Your Mindset:

- *Think about your passion. Research how to perfect your craft.*

- *Seek a mentor to inspire you to organize/prioritize your plans and thoughts.*

- *Execute your biggest play 1ˢᵗ that will produce the most income (If you have multiple plays in mind).*

N<small>OTES</small>:

Knowledge is Priceless & Powerful.

Education is an Asset.

Recondition Your Mindset & Secure the Bag.

✓ *Identify the Bag*

✓ *Get the Bag*

✓ *Secure the Bag*

✓ *Repeat.*

Secure The Bag

CHAPTER

SIX

J.O.B [JUST OVER BROKE]

● ● ● ● ● ● ● ● ●

CHAPTER SIX

J.O.B. [JUST OVER BROKE]

A job is a temporary form of consistent income for a short or long period, depending on the type of job and your status on the job. It is never for a lifetime or something you can pass down to your children or grandchildren to inherit. You will only get this income if you are willing to go and physically able to work. If suddenly you get sick or did not plan to miss work, you are done (your income that is). There goes you living paycheck-to-paycheck, that check you relied on is gone.

There are three different classes of people...the Poor, Middle, & Wealthy Class. These 3 different classes of people, all spend their money on different things on 'payday'. Which category do you fit in?

The Poor Class spends their money on just "stuff" or things that they want. The Middle Class spend their money on liabilities and struggle by thinking they're doing the right thing with their money. The

Wealthy Class spends their money on assets. Things that are going to make them more money whether it's now or in the future. Such as education, if you get a college degree you will be able to make more money in your field versus a person without a college degree.

A few others spend their money on investments and building businesses. Now, the only time a job is not Just Over Broke is when you make enough to invest, save, pay bills and enjoy life. In the words of Benjamin Franklin "Make more than you spend, and you have a recipe for happiness. Spend more than you make, and you will have a recipe for misery." **Let's turn J.O.B (Just Over Broke) into J.O.B (Jumpstart Our Business)!** Turn the negative into a positive.

Empowerment Techniques to Recondition Your Mindset:

- *Practice changing your mindset. Believe that Wealth is a Mind$et!*

- *Put together your budget sheet to see how much money is coming in and going out.*

- *Cut out any unnecessary spending habits.*

- *Research an investment company and start investing.*

N OTES:

Knowledge is Priceless & Powerful.

Education is an Asset.

Recondition Your Mindset & Secure the Bag.

✓ *Identify the Bag*

✓ *Get the Bag*

✓ *Secure the Bag*

✓ *Repeat.*

Secure The Bag

CHAPTER

SEVEN

TAKE THE RISK, INVEST

● ● ● ● ● ● ● ● ●

CHAPTER SEVEN

TAKE THE RISK, INVEST

I would rather see you invest and gain the chance to double your money or gain interest before I see you just blow your money on nonsense. Just think about how much money you invest in the material things

such as a pair of $200+ Jordans, oh don't let you be the type that wants to get them before everyone else and spend $250 or better on them. It's the urgency for me that got me like what, just to have them before they hit the store. What's going on in the minds of the urban communities, you still won't be the 1st one with them because you're not the only one that made that foolish move. Some even buy them for babies that can't even walk yet, and they are too big sometimes but the parents don't care because they're Jordan's, that's all that matters to them, "The Drip".

It's plenty of other things that I can give you an example of, but I'm sure you get it. If you like Jordan's so much, invest in them, get money with them. The Nike stock is less than the shoe itself, today's price is $167.79 for one share. See the ones that have those rich vibes will choose to get money with the company not give them their money or at least be in the position to do both.

During the pandemic, especially when it first hit there was a lot of relief from bill payments, PPE loans floating around, and IRS stimulus checks were sent out and still are. With all of the benefits of the pandemic there should be some money saved, invested or a business started to have something to show for yourself with all that free money, as some would call it. But most just blew through it. I'm guilty of blowing through some bands myself but I do also have some things to show for it. I gained some new experiences and have tried some new business adventures.

On another note, I do like that the urban community is coming along, with investing and making business moves more than ever before. I give social media the credit for ones that do want to learn, gain from the positive, seek knowledge and decide to follow positive influencers! Many were put onto Dogecoin & AMC just to name a few and was making a lot of noise amongst the urban communities. Now those were some conversations worth having for me "it was the stimulating the mental for me".

One of the 7th and biggest pillars of wealth is in Real Estate. You shall consider investing in properties. If you need to partner up with someone, form a joint venture, you can't go wrong with Real Estate investing, it's just the time of the market and location that will always be the biggest factors. You just need to know when to get in and when to get out. For instance, look at how crazy the market went through the roof during COVID-19. Most thought because it was a pandemic that everything was going to cease. Instead, homeowners' property values went up tremendously and everyone wanted to either buy or sell.

While it is extremely more challenging to rent it is more than enough reasons to just purchase a home. Buyback the block! Remember Nipsey Hustle, R.I.P., he purchased the store that he used to hustle in front of. That was a smart come-back move. When you purchase a home, you don't have to worry about a background check, which for many in the urban community is the reason you can't qualify to rent an apartment or house. You must jump through more hurdles just to rent, which you are the one paying someone else's investment off. That's kind of backward if you asked me.

Take the risk. "Scared money don't make money"! You should start investing as soon as today! Stop procrastinating. Prepare for tomorrow. Seek an investment professional also known as an asset manager. You will soon be able to consider yourself an investor, if you are willing to take the risk you may see larger gains.

A fundamental idea in finance is the relationship between risk and return. The greater the amount of risk that an investor is willing to take on, the greater the potential return. The reason for this is that investors need to be compensated for taking on additional risks. Gain the financial knowledge you need to succeed in the investing lane.

For instance, I took the risk when I invested $13,000K cash in order to predict getting $3000k a month, with a cleaning franchise company. Now that was a business move and an investment. I invested my money in this franchise hoping that the cleaning contracts would stay afloat. My husband and I took another risk when we invested in multiple vehicles to put on the Turo car-sharing platform to make money instead of gradually blowing our money. I rather double up my money than let my money sit in a regular bank account for that little bitty interest that the bank gives you for using your money to make money by letting their bank customers and investors borrow it and collect a way bigger interest than they give you.

The risk was that at any time I could have lost a contract or two. However, I got a few good years out of the deal. Though I lost a few contracts due to the recession back in 2008, companies reduced their cleaning contracts. I was proud of my investment and the experience. I made some good money for quite some time. With this investment, I had gained and then some lost. But this did not stop me from investing again.

Broadly speaking, there are three main reasons why an individual might wish to save and invest.

1st- The reason is to protect their hard-earned money and ensure its safety.
2nd- The reason is to generate current income which is passive income.

3rd- The reason is a desire to grow their principal and achieve capital gains.

Once an investor has experienced a substantial loss, it becomes increasingly difficult to meet their financial goals. A simple example will provide evidence as to why investors need to protect their principal. If a portfolio loses 50% of its principal, an investor must then generate gains of 100% just to reach the breakeven point. Given long-term averages for various investment classes, 100% gains can take years or even decades to achieve.

This does not mean that investors should avoid taking any losses at all. All investments contain some risk; the key to success is to identify an appropriate risk tolerance and then manage the portfolio to that tolerance. In some instances, this may mean that the avoidance of any losses is appropriate, but in others, moderate capital losses may be tolerable if the portfolio is properly designed to meet its long-term return objectives.

It Takes Money to Make Money

"Don't fear investing; educate yourself on your options." Saving and investing is a cycle. A cycle that helps you to build a sound financial portfolio. Understanding the power of saving and investing is important as it continuously takes money to make more money.

Invest Save, Repeat, Invest Save...

Empowerment Techniques to Recondition Your Mindset:

▪ *Research & connect with an asset manager.*

▪ *Learn about the different portfolios.*

▪ *Be wise and maybe start conservative until you get comfortable.*

▪ *If you are less than the age of 55 you should invest aggressively up to ten years before you retire.*

NOTES:

Knowledge is Priceless & Powerful.

Education is an Asset.

Recondition Your Mindset & Secure the Bag.

✓ *Identify the Bag*

✓ *Get the Bag*

✓ *Secure the Bag*

✓ *Repeat.*

Secure The Bag

CHAPTER

EIGHT

ASSETS AND LIABILITIES

● ● ● ● ● ● ● ● ●

CHAPTER EIGHT

ASSETS AND LIABILITIES

Calculating your net worth helps you figure out where you are financially now. Expressed as a dollar amount, your net worth represents your financial health and is essentially the result of everything you have earned and spent up until now. While taking the time to calculate your net worth one time is helpful, what is beneficial is to make this calculation regularly so you can see trends in your overall financial health.

Your net worth is a snapshot of your finances. The picture will change slightly the next time you pay a bill and the next time you receive a paycheck. To determine your current magic number, the first step is to look at all your assets, which are anything of value that you own. Make a list of all these items and next to each, list the amount it's worth. These typically include:

Cash-- any physical currency and coins you have in the bank- all the money you have in savings, checking, or money market accounts, stocks, bonds, certificates of deposit (CDs) and don't forget and any crypto that you may have.

Retirement accounts -- includes 401(k) funds, IRAs, and any other retirement accounts.

Life insurance -- counting any cash value you have in the policy.

Motor Vehicles-- the current blue book value of any cars, motorcycles, boats, trailers, RVs, etc.

Real Estate -- the current market value of the property (house, condo, land, etc.) you own, even if you have a mortgage.

Personal Valuables -- including the market value of jewelry, collectibles (from baseball cards to art), and furniture.

The money you're owed -- if you have a reasonable expectation of being paid back.

Just because you own these assets doesn't

mean you'll be able to access their monetary value today. Only cash and other highly liquid assets— things that you can exchange for a good market value quickly—are easily accessible. Although it might take months to turn real estate into its true cash value, use the full market value when calculating your net worth today. If you're unsure of what something

you own is worth—like an antique, find a professional appraiser.

When you're done listing assets, make a separate list of liabilities and amounts. Liabilities are any debts or payments you owe to someone else. Here are the most common:

Mortgage -- the principal or amount you have left to pay on your mortgage(s).

Home equity loan -- how much you owe if you have a home equity loan.

Automobile loan -- the amount you have yet to pay on your car(s) and other motor vehicles.

Student loans -- the amount left on student loans.

Credit card debt -- any balance owed to a credit card company.

Assets & Liabilities

What are Assets?

Assets are:

Bank Accounts

Investment Accounts

Deferred Annuity Accounts

Retirement Accounts

Business Assets

Real Estate and Residence

_____

_____

_____

_____

What are Liabilities?

Liabilities are:

Loans for Rental Property

Loans for Business

Furniture Rental Loans

Taxes

_____

_____

_____

_____

Empowerment Techniques to Recondition Your Mindset:

▪ *What would you like for your net worth to be? Whatever that number is, work towards getting it there!*

▪ *Once you're finished listing all your assets and liabilities, calculate the magic number.*

▪ *Realize your needs vs. wants. This will help you gain more assets.*

N OTES:

Knowledge is Priceless & Powerful.

Education is an Asset.

Recondition Your Mindset & Secure the Bag.

✓ *Identify the Bag*

✓ *Get the Bag*

✓ *Secure the Bag*

✓ *Repeat.*

Secure The Bag

CHAPTER

NINE

HOW MONEY WORKS

● ● ● ● ● ● ● ● ●

CHAPTER NINE

HOW MONEY WORKS

All school students should be required to take a class in financial education. When I published the 1st edition of this book back in 2015 only a handful of states have adopted degrees of the financial literacy curriculum. Only four states require high school students to take a semester-long course in personal finance to graduate. Which was Virginia, Missouri, Tennessee, and Utah. Since then, there are now 21 states that require financial literacy to graduate. So, studies show that it was well needed and worth the change.

Now as we all know we should not just leave it up to the educators to try and teach our children everything. Parents shall discuss how money works as a topic at the dinner table. Another suggestion is that parents can use back-to-school shopping as an opportunity to lay the foundation for helping their children develop sound money management habits early in life. You can also practice budgeting and how money works when it is Christmas shopping time! But only if you have big children that no longer believe in Santa Claus! Lol!

We can't claim to be preparing children for the future if we are not providing them with future survival skills.

Smartphone Apps: One of the best tech tools to teach financial literacy is one most children already have – a smartphone. Studies recommend using an app like ShopSavvy to teach comparison shopping. Users can scan a product's barcode and instantly receive information on prices of the same product at nearby stores and the Web.

One key fact is everyone must deal with money. It doesn't matter what career you choose or if you don't go to college. Everyone must deal with money. It is so basic, and it is so essential. It's only money, after all, that's just what we use to buy the things we need and want.

Children are usually just taught to get paid by employers, and use that money to pay the bills, buy food, and purchase goods and services, and then put some in a savings account at the bank. Currency seems like a straightforward concept. Money was invented and we use it, yet we cannot understand its laws or control its actions. It has a life of its own.

Empowerment Techniques to Recondition Your Mindset:

▪ *Set realistic budgets before you go shopping. Be clear as to your need vs. your want.*

▪ *Have your children prepare budgets with you and show them discipline in using the budget.*

▪ *Encourage them to follow the budget sheet and if they get an item more expensive that might mean sacrificing something else.*

▪ *Teach children ways to cut costs and manage cash flow, like clipping coupons, looking for sales, and comparing prices. (Some people make money off couponing).*

NOTES:

Knowledge is Priceless & Powerful.

Education is an Asset.

Recondition Your Mindset & Secure the Bag.

✓ *Identify the Bag*

✓ *Get the Bag*

✓ *Secure the Bag*

✓ *Repeat.*

Secure The Bag

Wealth is a Mind$et 2nd Edition by SHYNNA MITCHELL

CHAPTER

TEN

HOW CREDIT WORKS

● ● ● ● ● ● ● ● ●

CHAPTER TEN

HOW CREDIT WORKS

When I was 18 years old, I had a credit score of 680. Back then that was darn good! I was in great shape to purchase my first home and a brand-new car. Credit rules everything around you. If you haven't figured that out yet, well here you have it!

There was a time when my life took a left turn and went for a spin. In 2018, I had to shake some things up and shift some things around due to a bad marriage and got a divorce. I even had filed for bankruptcy and did a voluntary foreclosure on a property in my past before that life-changing event. Then I had to shake all those bad vibes and energy off and keep it moving. YES, I had to start over, but it didn't take me long at all to get it back up because I have always been motivated and determined.

Now, here I am still standing in 2021 remarried, new house, capital, and multiple cars amongst my husband and me. I have what the creditors consider an A-1 credit score. I can get anything I want and that sure feels good. I want it, I get it! If your credit score is at least 700, your supper straight. So, get your score up!

Your credit score determines if you can buy a house, rent a house, an apartment; get certain jobs, student loans, personal loans, or a car, whether you put a down payment for utility companies, and even how much you pay for car insurance.

Your score not only determines if you can get these items but even how much you will pay for them. The interest rate is what makes that difference in the price you pay. If you've read how credit reports work, you know that your credit report contains a history of how you've paid your bills, how much open credit you have, if you went over your credit limit, and anything else that would affect your creditworthiness.

Your credit score boils down all that information to a three-digit number. Using the credit score, lenders can predict with some accuracy how likely the borrower is to repay a loan and make payments on time. It's how creditors can offer instant credit.

There are several scoring methods; most lenders use the FICO method from Fair Isaac Corporation. Each of the three major credit bureaus is Experian, Equifax, and TransUnion. A credit score is determined much like a grade in school. Consider how a teacher calculates grades by taking scores from tests, homework, attendance, and anything else they want to use, weighing each one according to importance to come up with a final, single-number score. It's the same for a credit score.

But, instead of using the scores from pop quizzes and papers, it uses the information on your credit report. The number ranges from 300 to 850. Although the exact formula for calculating the score is proprietary information and owned by Fair Isaac, here's an approximate breakdown of how it is determined: 35 percent of the score is based on your payment history.

This makes sense since one of the primary

reasons a lender wants to see the score is to find out if and how promptly you pay your bills. The score is affected by how many bills have been paid late, how many were sent out for collection, and if you have ever filed for bankruptcy. When these things happen also comes into play. The more recent, the worse it will be for your overall score; thirty percent of the score is based on outstanding debt.

How much do you owe on a car or home loan? How many credit cards do you have that are at their credit limits? The more cards you have at their limits, the lower your score will be. The rule of thumb is to keep your card balances at 30 percent or less of their credit limits.

Fifteen percent of the score is based on the length of time you've had credit. The longer you've had established credit, the better it is for your overall credit score. Why? Because more information about your past payment history gives a more accurate prediction of your future actions.

Ten percent of the score is based on new credit. Opening new credit accounts will negatively affect your score for a short time. This category also penalizes hard inquiries on your credit in the past year. Hard inquiries are when you've permitted lenders to pull your credit, as opposed to soft inquiries, which include looking at your own score which does not affect your score. However, the score interprets several hard inquiries within a short amount of time as one hard inquiry to allow consumers to shop around for the best loan.

Ten percent of the score is based on the types of credit you currently have. It will help your score to show that you have had experience with several different kinds of credit accounts, such as revolving credit accounts and installment loans. This information is compared to the credit performance of other consumers with similar histories and profiles.

The three major credit bureaus each have their version of the credit score, all of which are based on the original Fair Isaac scoring method. Equifax has the BEACON system, TransUnion has the classic FICO Risk Score system, and Experian has the Experian/Fair Isaac RISK system. Some lenders also have their scoring methods, which may include information such as your income or how long you've been at the same job.

Paying your bills on time or 'before-time is also very important to your creditworthiness.

Example:

A calendar with all the bill due dates is a helpful tool for success in your financial life.

Electric	$250	due 05/08/2022
Car Payment	$700	due 05/25/2022
Car Insurance	$130	due 05/15/2022

Make sure you are consistent with the dates on which you pay your bills. The same bills should be paid with the same payroll check each month to prevent oversight—that may cost you late fees.

Better yet auto-pay is what your monthly bills should be on. You know every month, the same bills come back around. Auto-pay frees up time from you having to remember to pay bills every month.

Empowerment Techniques to Recondition Your Mindset:

▪ *Visit www.annualcreditreport.com to get your free credit report. You are entitled to one free credit report once a year. Also, you can purchase your credit score from all 3 credit bureaus.*

▪ *Check your credit report for inaccuracies. If there are any, dispute them.*

▪ *If there are any items on your report that are more than 7 years old, contact the credit bureaus and tell them to delete the item from your report.*

▪ *Do not ever close a credit account. That harms your credit score. Just cut the card up if you don't want to use it anymore.*

NOTES:

Knowledge is Priceless & Powerful.

Education is an Asset.

Recondition Your Mindset & Secure the Bag.

✓ *Identify the Bag*

✓ *Get the Bag*

✓ *Secure the Bag*

✓ *Repeat.*

Secure The Bag

CHAPTER

ELEVEN

LIVING THE LIFE

● ● ● ● ● ● ● ● ●

CHAPTER ELEVEN

LIVING LIFE

Whatever happened to living the typical American dream being the household conversation? The conversations generally would be the parents encouraging their children to go to college, get a job, establish good credit, save and buy a house by the time you're the age of 30 in order to have your house paid off by the time of retirement. Those were back in the day, good old conversations.

Now of days conservations hit a lot different. There is so much more to life that the urban communities have caught wind of, such as entrepreneurship and business startups. Things were kept from the urban community for the most part or put in a book because others thought that most in the urban community don't read therefore most would be late catching on and learning about more ways to get ahead in life.

So set those typical goals above and look forward to them the moment you graduate from high school. Once you start living your life, don't let the typical 'Okie Dokie' excuses for poor financial behavior kick in such as the sayings of YOLO (You Only Live Once) or Fear of Missing Out (FOMO). These poor financial behaviors if not corrected will mess up your whole life. Be exceptional, not ordinary.

As mentioned early on I had purchased my first home at the age of 26! At that time, I had good credit and a job! However, things didn't always stay afloat. I did take a hit when the economy went down, and the recession hit in 2008. I had some setbacks at that time, but I did continue to work on my comeback.

The typical American Dream is the idea that Americans can secure a better material life for themselves through hard work. The American Dream is much more than a house, two children, and a car in the garage. It's also the idea that Americans can strive for a life of proud individualism, recognition, and personal liberty.

If there's one thing about, ''living the life'', that most can agree on, that it requires hard work to achieve. Most appreciate things more when they, "get it out of the mud". Whether you're aiming to climb from humble beginnings to a comfortable middle-class life, ascend from the middle class to the upper class, or even climb from the very bottom to the highest echelons of society, you'll need a powerful personal drive to succeed.

Getting ahead in life means what it sounds like, working hard so that you pull ahead of others who would rather put in only the bare minimum level of effort. For starters, you may want to try working smarter and longer than other people at your job. Notice I said smarter not harder. If most employees usually leave soon as it's time to clock out, offer to stay late. If others slack during their downtime, find extra tasks to do. Working smarter than other people around you is an excellent way to get noticed at work and eventually reap the rewards of promotion and raises.

While America is home to many people with stories who became successful without a formal education, getting an education is usually a big boost to your career and personal growth. A basic education, like you, get from high school, gives most the baseline knowledge you need to be mediocre in the world.

A higher education, like you, get at college, gives you specialized knowledge and skills which make you a more attractive candidate and qualify for more selective jobs, while a post-graduate education is even more specialized. It's best to get the highest level of education you can reasonably afford.

When you know better, you do better. Hopefully, making you beware of the dangers of your financial moves, will encourage you. If you're not the type to make big goals or have big dreams, I do encourage you to reach the most typical goals, so that you and your family can the least have a decent and stable lifestyle.

Empowerment Techniques to Recondition Your Mindset:

- *Get the highest education you can to secure a career or become a business owner.*

- *Your focus is to secure a good stable life.*

- *Find ways to work smarter not harder.*

- *Become a homeowner instead of a renter.*

- *Every dollar saved contributes to your bottom line.*

NOTES:

Knowledge is Priceless & Powerful.

Education is an Asset.

Recondition Your Mindset & Secure the Bag.

✓ *Identify the Bag*

✓ *Get the Bag*

✓ *Secure the Bag*

✓ *Repeat.*

Secure The Bag

CHAPTER

TWELVE

THE BENEFITS OF HOMEOWNERSHIP vs. RENTING

● ● ● ● ● ● ● ● ●

CHAPTER TWELVE

THE BENEFITS OF HOMEOWNERSHIP vs. RENTING

If you have a stable career and have been on your job for at least two years, I will say go for it! Become a first-time homeowner! I recommend being on your job for at least two years for the simple reason of being a little seasoned. You should know that you're comfortable with your career and gain the feeling that you will be there for a while.

Even though the Mortgage lenders usually require the least, 6 months of employment on a new job, a good credit score of at least 580 in the past, and a 3.5% down payment. Since the pandemic, lenders have increased the minimum credit score to be 640 for FHA and VA with a 3.5% down payment. For USDA, Jumbo, and Conventional loan products, the minimum score requirement is 660 and the down payments vary with these loan programs.

There are some, first-time homeowner programs that have down payment assistance. Even though in this unique housing market, you wouldn't stand a chance submitting an offer with down payment assistance. Buyers with loans that include the down payment assistance program take longer to close and tend to have more risk than a buyer that doesn't need the down payment assistance. Therefore, the seller will bypass that offer with the down payment assistance if the seller has multiple offers.

Also, there are rent-to-own programs that allow you to rent-to-own home with a credit score low as 550-credit score. Then once your credit score goes up, you can purchase the home from the program. On the other hand, Neighborhood Assistance Corporation of America (NACA) doesn't even rely on credit scores.

Throughout my 13 years of practicing Real Estate and even life within itself, I became big on being in the "knowing business". My suggestion to our clients is to take the speculation out of the equation. Have less worry about your credit status and just apply for the mortgage loan to obtain a solution.

Let the mortgage lender tell you exactly what you need to work on if anything at all. Don't allow a credit repair company to sell you on their credit repair program. Those programs are long drawn out to collect a monthly fee and to attempt to wipe everything from your credit reports and that's not necessary.

You see, the credit repair companies are in business to make money not to close on a home, which when the lender close on a home, that's when the lender gets paid. The lender has an end game. So, the credit repair companies will drag you along, the long way. They have no end game. The mortgage company does not make money off telling what you need to do to boost your credit score, they make money once you close on your home. Therefore, their trajectory is straightforward, on a fast track to get you to the closing table as soon as possible.

The mortgage company, your real estate agent and you are all on the same page, same end game that works in your best interest. The credit repair companies can care less if you close on a new home or not, they're getting their money already upfront.

The benefit of being a homeowner is that you are stable. You don't have to worry about landlord rules or better yet a slumlord. The landlord makes money off the renter. The rent amount is way higher than the mortgage amount the landlord pays to their lender, in which you are ultimately helping pay off their investment.

During the pandemic, landlords had the opportunity to apply for a pandemic mortgage relief, which allowed them to have extensions of 3 months plus to make their mortgage payment. On the other hand, sadly they still expected to collect the rent from tenants, capitalizing on the unfortunate circumstances whether the tenants were still employed or not. Thank God there was a freeze put in place on the filings of evictions and rent relief to protect the tenants.

Being a landlord is just business to them. Remember, to make money and you paying off their investment. When you have the upper hand, you have the leverage to get the most out of situations. If you decide to take advantage and operate in that manner, in any situation with no sympathy or bending when adjustments can be made, especially when adjustments have been made (for the landlords) when they didn't even have to pay their mortgage. That's greed.

Landlords usually don't work with you too much if anything happens with your finances, such as during the pandemic, a layoff, or on medical leave. An eviction is filed. You're messing up their business. Once you can no longer pay, you're no longer able to stay.

Now on the flip side, if you are the homeowner, you have the authority to negotiate with the mortgage company if you are experiencing a qualifying hardship. Mortgage companies would rather negotiate and keep you in your home versus accumulating another foreclosure on their books to try and resale and lose more money. Mortgage Companies may be a little more flexible to work with than big banks.

Also, another benefit to homeownership is that your mortgage payment will be much less than you would pay rent for that same house. You will save money and secure a stable living environment for your family for many years until you decide to make a change if ever desired.

I have been on the 3 sides of the fence. I was a renter that had to deal with a slumlord. I was the homeowner that had to deal with tenants in my rental property that had to file for evictions and fix damages. Also, was a homeowner that enjoyed being a homeowner.

Homeownership vs. Renting

(H) Fixed monthly payments.

(R) Fluctuating rent fees yearly.

Possibility of selling for profit.

(R) No profit.

(H) Set your own rules for your peace & enjoyment.

(R) The landlord determines rules.

(H) Renovations can increase property value.

(R) If you make certain changes to the property, the landlord can require you to change it back or deduct it from your security deposit.

(H) Mortgage companies work with homeowners during hardships.

(R) Landlords file an eviction if you experience hardship and do not have the funds to pay.

Legend: (H)= Homeowner (R)= Renter

Empowerment Techniques to Recondition Your Mindset:

▪ *Being a homeowner between the ages of 21-35 helps to pay off your home by retirement.*

▪ *Go for something modest and find a great deal.*

▪ *Consider purchasing a fixer-upper, a foreclosure, or a HUD property, their much cheaper but can be turn out to be lovely, renovated homes; or a multi-unit so the one unit can pay the mortgage and you live mortgage-free.*

▪ *Save money for closing costs and a down payment just in case there are no available funds or programs at the time or within the county in which you want to purchase a property. (Which in this 2021 market, don't even think about a down payment program, you won't stand a chance with the bidding wars. This method will only come back into play when it becomes a buyer's mark again).*

NOTES:

Knowledge is Priceless & Powerful.

Education is an Asset.

Recondition Your Mindset & Secure the Bag.

✓ *Identify the Bag*

✓ *Get the Bag*

✓ *Secure the Bag*

✓ *Repeat.*

Secure The Bag

CHAPTER

THIRTEEN

HOW GRATITUDE CAN CHANGE YOUR LIFE

● ● ● ● ● ● ● ● ●

CHAPTER THIRTEEN

HOW GRATITUDE CAN CHANGE YOUR LIFE

In life and throughout it all, I have learned to be grateful and to appreciate what I already have and accomplished. By practicing this, the abundance of more is overflowing! I practice the law of attraction, speaking what I want into existence, and thanking God for what yet is to come. Whatever you focus on or keep thinking about you will end up manifesting it unconsciously. Be careful of your thoughts, they become words and actions eventually. Your mind is powerful. Use it wisely! One good thought in the morning will set the tone for your whole day!

I felt the need to share this thought process with you, as it has helped me. Now, I didn't always use this thought process. When I moved to Atlanta, GA from Buffalo, NY within the first year, I bought my first rental property, a franchise, sold real estate, living in a nice big home, and drove a seven-passenger Audi Q7 truck with the panoramic sunroof! Sounds very intriguing right! Well, it was a wonderful feeling while it lasted. I say that because I had gotten a little 'big-headed' and took for granted all the wonderful things I acquired and accomplished in such a short period.

My attitude was, I can always get those things. I took the material things for granted and things took a left turn during the recession period that hit in 2008. I was so distraught. One thing left at a time. I was like... "Wow!" And of course, it wasn't as easy as I thought it would be to regain that status back. Once I had that experience it changed my life forever. I learned to think differently and most of all, I began to have more gratitude.

I love to empower people from my personal, real-life experiences and use them as testimonies. If you fall it's 'okay' if you still have your legs and feet, you can stand back up! Don't be afraid. Businesses go under and life changes happen, and you can bounce back up with a different strategy.

I applied this same thinking process and pattern when I decided to get a divorce in 2018 and went through the rebuilding process. When I say rebuilding process, I mean even mentally even though I was the petitioner. It's a natural process you go through, I must admit no matter if you're the petitioner or the respondent I believe.

I had to get up and dust the dirt off my shoulders, I grabbed part of the woman I was once before, such as my pure, general nurturing caring ways and ambition back but also left behind part of the monster that I felt I had become; by being involved in a very toxic, domestic, verbal, and financially abusive marriage. It didn't sit well with my spirit and soul, that I had started acting out in ways that I should not have, as a reaction to my ex's actions. For the first time in my life, I felt under attack, under a dark cloud, and went into a dark space.

I woke up one day, got out of that

dark space. Thank God, the counseling sessions, the prayer room, listening to motivational YouTubes video's half of the day at work; some of which my Queen Mother had shared with me. The other half of the day I switched over to this one IG comedian, all to help me get out of that dark space.

I knew I couldn't do it alone and was very private and careful in seeking counsel. All counsel is not wise counsel, so didn't disclose what I was going through to, many family members or friends. I didn't want any more confusion, I just wanted out, a solution, to sit still, in order to gain clarity and to hear God speak to me. So, that day I decided enough is enough. My poor choice of that male selection was nothing but another self-inflicting injury. I knew better, all the signs were there. I had run into the same cycle that I had a few other times before in my past which was a pattern, a cycle, just different scenery. "If you keep going into the same cycle you won't get anywhere different". In the words of

Sadhguru, one of my YouTube influencers.

I started indulging in my business adventures again, focused on my children more since they had to go through healing also, believe that. Claiming and speaking the new type of man that I learned that I desired and wanted to lead in my children and I life, my ideal King, I made room for him by not letting anyone temporarily fill that seat on the throne, keeping that side of the closet open, that side of the bed empty, etc.… Your King can't come with a boy toy in the way!

Then my King had arrived. I had spoken my ideal man, new house, new car, becoming a full-time Realtor and God gave me even more than I asked for! Overflow!

I took my time; meaning I didn't go with the ones that wanted me. I selected the one that I wanted, that my soul, energy, connection, and prayer had led me to first and foremost. Once I sensed my husband, I did the selecting this time by agreeing with the type of character of a man who I consciously decided to let into my space. I was happily able to share my good energy and love again. So, once I noticed my husband was who I prayed for, I selected, let him tell it, lol, nawh, we were both on the same page. It panned out lovely with human trial and error which occurs while building any new foundation.

There's no blueprint to life. Never expect perfection or try to be. You will set yourself up for failure and fail every time. What I meant by that, I selected this time; in the past, I had let the wrong ones select me without me doing my due diligence. When you're a good solid catch of course you'll be wanted by many.

I must admit, I kept running into the same type of guys and same lifestyle cycle. At, that point in time, in my life, I wasn't ready for a different lifestyle and a real man. A few had crossed my path, but to be honest, I was intimidated and wasn't used to anything other than the young woman perspective that I had gathered on my own about guys but clearly, I had it wrong.

I lost my father when I was 15 due to murder and my brother at the age of 17 due to a 65-year prison sentence. The most important men in my life that I was raised in the household with, my male influencers, and role models were suddenly gone. So, dang, I let the wrong ones select me. However, I believe I had to go through those life experiences to teach me how to appreciate a King.

Every move you make is like a chess game; you must make your next move your best move. If you have a bad thought hurry and change that thought. Turn that negative energy into a positive. Think about something positive to put a smile on your face. It's not the end of the world long as God woke you up you can try again!

Once you get where you feel you want to be in life and accomplish your goals, don't ever look back or "toot your nose up" at others. Just as fast God blessed you with it, God can take it away from you.

//Don't burn bridges with people.

Even if the only thing you say is "Thank You", that would suffice. Gratitude shifts your focus from what your life lacks to the abundance that is already present. In addition, behavioral and psychological research has shown the surprising life improvements can stem from the practice of gratitude. Giving thanks makes people happier, strengthens relationships, improves health, and reduces stress. Research also shows gratitude heightens the quality of life. So, in other words, this goes so much further than just my personal experience.

There are so many ways to practice gratitude. You can practice gratitude by writing down just a few things a day that you are grateful for. Say "thank you" for the money you haven't received yet. Be grateful for the business adventure or job you are seeking. Say "thank you" for your terrific relationship with your husband/wife, even if you don't have one yet. Just know your thoughts are powerful and you are attracting want you are and what you want!

Speak Everything You Desire into Existence and Enjoy the NOW Moments!

Empowerment Techniques to Recondition Your Mindset:

- *Say thank you, thank you, thank you 3 times for all things that come your way, whether it is a good or a bad experience so now you know what to look out for or avoid next time. Always know that it could be worse.*

- *Don't burn bridges.*

- *Don't become 'big-headed' once you get where you want to be.*

- *Remember gratitude, prayer, faith, and work will carry you a long way!*

N OTES:

Knowledge is Priceless & Powerful.
Education is an Asset.
Recondition Your Mindset & Secure the Bag.

✔ *Identify the Bag*

✔ *Get the Bag*

✔ *Secure the Bag*

✔ *Repeat.*

Secure The Bag

About the Author

SHYNNA MITCHELL

The Financial Fanatic Financial & Business
Empowerment Coach/Author /Speaker/Realtor

SHYNNA MITCHELL
was born Shynna McCown, in New Haven, CT. Her
family moved to Buffalo, NY in 1993 when she was
11. Now she resides near Atlanta, GA with her
husband and children.

Shynna has been through some real trauma in her
past. At age 15 her father was murdered, 2 yrs. later
at age 17, she lost her brother to a 65-year prison
sentence. One year later she got married at the age
of 18 and started experiencing domestic violence
and living the lifestyle of "good girls like bad boys"
which resulted in 2 failed marriages. She still stood
strong.

Throughout it all, Shynna is remarried and has
managed to become a financial realist who has
always had a knack for encouraging others despite
her experiences. With well over 19 years of
financial experience within the Real Estate,
Mortgage Industries, Corporate America, Operated
and Owned a Commercial Cleaning Business, she
brings much to the table to digest when it comes to
empowering and educating individuals regarding
reconditioning your mindset of wealth building with

multiple streams of income.

Throughout the years, her advice and coaching have touched many lives in the areas such as Finances, Entrepreneurship, Budgeting, Credit, Investing, and Multiple Streams of Income. She strongly believes that presenting information in an easy-to-understand manner helps to provide a relatable catalyst to aid in long-term wealth-building success.

SHYNNA MITCHELL's mission as The Financial Fanatic/Strategist is to empower the 'Now & Ready' to become aware and obtain this knowledge as they travel along the road to long-term Financial Freedom.

The Financial Fanatic

"Though my life has its ups-and-downs, I appreciate each moment within my journey. These days, I feel blessed to be able to share my knowledge, experience, and God-given talents with the world."

Shynna is also a member of the Atlanta's Women Entrepreneurs (AWE), Atlanta's Urban Professional, and shares her time/resources through volunteerism, philanthropic efforts, and support of community financial literacy initiatives.

"With her Empowerment, you will learn to love your new relationship with your finances!"

To book SHYNNA MITCHELL for speaking engagements, community events, or other outreach opportunities, Email: info@wealthisamindset.org

Website: wealthisamindset.org

Phone: 678-664-9774

Stay in tune, follow Shynna on

@shynnamitchell & @2SLMProperties

EDUCATION

EMPOWERMENT

REAL ESTATE SERVICE

MENTORSHIP

As a continued committed effort

SHYNNA MITCHELL seeks to join forces with other companies, organizations, and community/social groups to empower individuals within their financial lives regardless of 'where *they have been*' or '*what they are currently experiencing*'.

WHO ARE YOU FINANCIALLY?

EXPLORING YOUR FINANCIAL LIFE FROM THE INSIDE OUT

Financial/Business Empowerment Coach,

SHYNNA MITCHELL

OBJECTIVE: To assist in/or fully facilitate ongoing outreach events and programs for women & men seeking to change or grow within their financial lives by empowering them with information, encouraging goal-setting, and discussing various financial options.

Invite SHYNNA MITCHELL to host a Wealth is a Mind$et session at your workplace, social setting, etc.

Contact Information Email:info@wealthisamindset.org

Website: wealthisamindset.org

▪ PROFESSIONAL COACHING SERVICES ▪ BOOKS ▪ EMPOWERING MENTORSHIP

Community & corporate organizations, entertainment industry platforms, local gathering venues, social networks.

Amazon, Barnes & Noble, Book Signing Tours, Author Private Events Seminars/Informational Sessions, Retail Stores [Local & Online] Customer Referral Network, Industry Network, Community Outreach, Colleges & University Events, Wedding/Bridal Events, Print Media, Television & Radio Promotion Campaigns, Sponsorships, Author Connections/Conferences

Additional Markets: Canada and Europe Market

Inspiring Informational Seminars by
Financial/Business Empowerment Coach
SHYNNA MITCHELL
"Recondition Your Mindset"

(WITH SHYNNA MITCHELL)

Your financial life plays a huge role in your overall external happiness & success. Therefore, Financial/Business Empowerment Coach SHYNNA MITCHELL has set out to offer key one-on-one and group sessions to help "boost" your financial/business mindset.

Those that attend her empowering informational seminar sessions have come to know her as the 'The Financial Fanatic' because of her passion for financial education & empowerment as well as her caring 'realness' coaching style, and financial tips & techniques all of which are geared to enhance your financial life; helping individuals to become recondition their mindsets.

"Many of my clients have agreed that having a session helps to give them new & fresh financial ideas, tools, tips and overall empowers them to grow & look at building multiple streams of income with a different perspective than ever before."

SHYNNA MITCHELL has a strong passion for empowering individuals to recondition their mindsets.

The Financial Fanatic Financial & Business Empowerment Coach/Author /Speaker/Realtor

S H Y N N A M I T C H E L L

An inspiring author of empowerment that promotes the canons of financial growth for a lifetime.

****

Email the Author: info@wealthisamindset.org

To order bulk quantities or wholesale for retail send email requests to:

2SLMPublishing@gmail.com

Wealth is a Mindset
Shynna Mitchell
The Financial Fanatic | Author | Real Estate Agent | Investor
EMPOWERING YOU TO BUILD YOUR EMPIRE!
SUBSCRIBE & TURN ON NOTIFICATIONS
@shynnamitchell

● ● ● ● ● ● ● ● ●

Affirmation: Each day I am reconditioning my mindset to enhance my life.

Resources

Credit Did you know? You can receive your free credit report from each bureau once a year.

• Freecreditreport.com

• Creditkarma.com

• Experian.com

• Equifax.com

• Transunion.com

Insurance "Life insurance is a necessity. It helps to protect our family and our legacy." Business-Key Person Insurance- This insurance will ensure that your business assets are protected. It also helps to protect your business partners & employees in the event something happens to you.

Personal Life Insurance- Many people (especially younger individuals) do not consider the full benefits of having Life Insurance. Life insurance protects you and your family in the event the inevitable happens. Having a life insurance policy in place can help to ease your mind and alleviate the burden of funeral expenses and financial obligations from those who will be responsible for your final estate.

Business

Georgia Secretary of State: (or the SOS in your state)

• sos.ga.gov Secretary of state to incorporate your business or nonprofit organization. Sole Proprietor: A sole proprietor is someone who owns an unincorporated business by himself or herself. They take sole responsibility for any legal aspect that can affect them personally as well. LLC Corporation: This business can be one person or a partnership and, in this corporation, you are limited to any risk by only your initial investment. Other Business Designations are Nonprofit, Corporation, S-Corp, and C-Corp

Tax Identification

To Obtain a Tax Identification Number:

• **www.irs.gov**

Trademark

To Trademark your Business Logo:

• **www.uspto.gov**

The Small Business Administration

Register Your Business with The SBA:

• www.sba.gov The SBA will also help guide you as sculpt your business plan as well as give you information about grants and loans for your business

Other Useful Information

• Legalzoom: Service company that can help you if you are not able to walk yourself through the legal process of any part of the business aspect for low rates.

• Google.com: Google anything on how to start or do anything.

• Ehow.com: Great resource on how to start any productive business.

• www.businessplan.com: Guided business plans & general business forms.

• www.naca.com: Neighborhood Assistance Corporation of America (NACA) is a great resource for homebuyers to obtain mortgage information.

Real Estate Services

(Servicing the State of Georgia & Referral Services within the other 49 states)

Keller Williams Realty Atlanta Partners

303 Corporate Center Dr. Ste 100

Stockbridge, GA 30281

Agent Information: Shynna Mitchell

Office: 770-692-0888

Direct: 678-664-9774
2SLMProperties@gmail.com

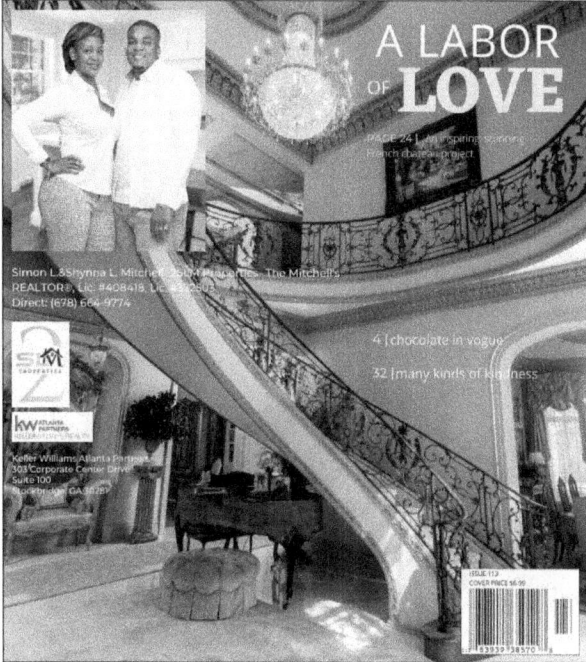

Compliments of Simon L.&Shynna L. Mitchell- 2SLM Properties- The Mitchell's

AMERICAN LIFESTYLE
THE MAGAZINE CELEBRATING LIFE IN AMERICA — ISSUE 113

Property Search Tools

• GAMLS.com

• FMLS.com

(These are the only 2 official residential real estate sites that Realtors use. These are not 3rd party sites. The properties that are listed on these sites are updated in real-time.)

Budget

• Mint.com- Analyze spending habits. The main thing to remember no matter what type of business that you decide to embark upon is ...the business must fund itself. Keep your personal finances separate from your business finances. So, be mindful of what and how much you are investing in your business so that you are clear when it comes to getting a full return on your investment. (ROI) Return on Investment.

Furnishing Options for Your Business- If you are starting a business with limited funds, start with the basics. Don't be ashamed to go to thrift stores, garage/estate sales, Facebook Marketplace, OfferUp, or business closing auctions to find office furnishings, decorative items, and even office supplies. You may be surprised at what you may find.

Technology/software, computers, printers, copy machines, etc. may all be things that you will need to get your business up and running—which can all be very pricey. Therefore, it is important to find out exactly what is needed to run your operation so that you don't "waste time and money". Then, once you have assessed the technology/software needed, it may be a great idea to do a 'three-bid' price comparison to ensure that you are not overspending. This is one of the most common failures of most small businesses... overspending. So, my advice would be—create a sense of financial awareness when it comes to budgeting your revenue and income. Also, to make sensible economical purchases for your business.

Marketing Be Resourceful... Find Start-up Low-Cost Marketing Resources D-I-Y Marketing (Do it Yourself)

These links are professional, inexpensive business material. Be creative—even on a budget.

• godaddy.com- Website builder

• freewebs.com- Beginner website builder

• vistaprint.com- Low-cost marketing materials such as business cards, flyers, brochures, etc.

Business Support Build a Knowledgeable, Passionate & Productive Support Team that has a clear focus and common goal of success.

The well-renowned business mogul Russell Simmons's accredited himself as a better businessman because of his staff, which he referred to as 'being smarter than him'— "I've been blessed to find people who are smarter than I am, and they help me to execute the vision I have."

Having a team of well-spirited, goal-oriented individuals with a similar 'smart work' ethic can help to send your business goals to their next level.

With a true team, goals turn into results and results continue to grow as your team grows. Some of the most successful business owners in the world may agree that being successful has everything to do with having a 'power team' to help support their business vision. *"It takes the support of a village to build a temple."*

And finally, it's all about ATTITUDE! "Your business is their business..."

Attitude is everything when it comes to winning in business. It is crucial to your business to have a team that shares that same winning attitude. When you decide to recruit members for your team, be sure to identify individuals that have mutual respect for your business vision—those that will treat the matters of your business seriously.

Businesses thrive primarily because their support team shares the organization's attitude of success. Having a team with a positive attitude of success in mind also helps to eliminate confusion so that ideals are communicated effectively to stay on course with the vision.

Reconditioned Mindset- Six Month Action Plan with Budget Sheet

■

The Reconditioned Mindset Challenge

■

To recondition your mindset, you must first be real with your current financial situation, educate yourself on ways to change, and take action! Here you will find a six-month action plan that will assist you as you seek to build your empire. Set aside a moment of your time monthly to go over your budget and a plan that is realistic to your lifestyle and watch your results!

...Set Goals ...Educate Yourself ...Become More Disciplined ...Have a Willingness to Sacrifice ...Exude Gratitude ...Give Back

Goal Setting Tips TO RECONDITION YOUR MINDSET

Our goals—big and small—help to shape the world around us and ultimately dictate our success in all areas of our lives.

The keys to effective goal setting:

1. Be specific about your goal.

Example: Simply writing ..."I want a new car." is a vague goal statement.

Instead, it may be more clear to say..."I want a white BMW X6."

2. Set a date for reaching this goal.

Example: "I will have it by May 15, 2022."

3. Develop a plan for reaching your goals.

Example: If your goal is...Through real estate investing, I will at least acquire two income-producing properties that will create a net cash flow of at least $500 per month each."

Then come up with a plan to make it happen...

a. Seek funding sources or speak with a Mortgage Professional.

b. Talk to a Real Estate Agent or Check your local listings for property in your area of interest.

c. Find out about city fees, codes, or regulations for renting your property.

HOW WILL I REACH MY GOALS?

The next question begins with HOW—"how do I achieve my goals?" Once you have written them down. Develop a plan on how you will achieve each goal. When you develop a plan, it should be of logical importance and include a schedule as to what you can accomplish first.

By prioritizing your goals, you have a better chance of becoming a lifetime achiever as setting priorities helps you to stay on course. It also helps you to get a full understanding of the 'who, what, when, and why's of your goal-setting mission. Thus, helping to solidify your plan, enabling you to overcome the obstacles that will come your way.

GOALS

To succeed, I must set clear goals for myself.

My top five Reconditioned Mindset Goals are:

1._____

Date I plan to achieve this goal: _____

2._____

Date I plan to achieve this goal: _____

3._____

Date I plan to achieve this goal: _____

4._____

Date I plan to achieve this goal: _____

5._____

Date I plan to achieve this goal: _____

EDUCATION

To succeed, I will educate myself in the areas in which I most need training & information so that I will achieve my goals.

My top five Reconditioned Mindset Education sources

1._____
2._____
3._____
4._____
5._____

Monthly Savings Goal:

$_____

Monthly Budget Sacrifice Item:

_____

Month_____

Monthly Plan of Action to Recondition My Mindset

_____

_____

_____

_____

_____

_____

_____

Income

Salary (1) $_____ Salary (2 $_____

Cash $_____

Child Support/Alimony $_____

Investment Income $_____

Other Income Resources $_____

Total $_____

Expenses

Rent/Mortgage $_____

Homeowners/Rental Insurance $_____

Utilities $_____

Internet/Cable/Telephone $_____

Transportation/Car Payment $_____

Child Care $_____

Insurance (Car) $_____

Insurance (Life/Disability/Medical) $_____

Groceries/Dining $_____

Clothing $_____

Entertainment $_____

Travel (Business/Personal) $_____

Education/Training $_____

Grooming (Hair/Nails) $_____

Savings/Retirement Plan $_____

Total $_____

Monthly Savings Goal:

$_____

Monthly Budget Sacrifice Item:

_____

Month_____

Monthly Plan of Action to Recondition My Mindset

_____

_____

_____

_____

_____

_____

_____

_____

Income

Salary (1) $_____ Salary (2 $_____

Cash $_____

Child Support/Alimony $_____

Investment Income $_____

Other Income Resources $_____

Total $_____

Expenses

Rent/Mortgage $_____

Homeowners/Rental Insurance $_____

Utilities $_____

Internet/Cable/Telephone $_____

Transportation/Car Payment $_____

Child Care $_____

Insurance (Car) $_____

Insurance (Life/Disability/Medical) $_____

Groceries/Dining $_____

Clothing $_____

Entertainment $_____

Travel (Business/Personal) $_____

Education/Training $_____

Grooming (Hair/Nails) $_____

Savings/Retirement Plan $_____

Total $_____

Monthly Savings Goal:

$_____

Monthly Budget Sacrifice Item:

_____

Month_____

Monthly Plan of Action to Recondition My Mindset

_____

_____

_____

_____

_____

_____

_____

_____

Income

Salary (1) $_____ Salary (2) $_____

Cash $_____

Child Support/Alimony $_____

Investment Income $_____

Other Income Resources $_____

Total $_____

Expenses

Rent/Mortgage $_____

Homeowners/Rental Insurance $_____

Utilities $_____

Internet/Cable/Telephone $_____

Transportation/Car Payment $_____

Child Care $_____

Insurance (Car) $_____

Insurance (Life/Disability/Medical) $_____

Groceries/Dining $_____

Clothing $_____

Entertainment $_____

Travel (Business/Personal) $_____

Education/Training $_____

Grooming (Hair/Nails) $_____

Savings/Retirement Plan $_____

Total $_____

Monthly Savings Goal:

$_____

Monthly Budget Sacrifice Item:

_____

Month_____

Monthly Plan of Action to Recondition My Mindset

_____

_____

_____

_____

_____

_____

_____

_____

Income

Salary (1) $_____ Salary (2) $_____

Cash $_____

Child Support/Alimony $_____

Investment Income $_____

Other Income Resources $_____

Total $_____

Expenses

Rent/Mortgage $_____

Homeowners/Rental Insurance $_____

Utilities $_____

Internet/Cable/Telephone $_____

Transportation/Car Payment $_____

Child Care $_____

Insurance (Car) $_____

Insurance (Life/Disability/Medical) $_____

Groceries/Dining $_____

Clothing $_____

Entertainment $_____

Travel (Business/Personal) $_____

Education/Training $_____

Grooming (Hair/Nails) $_____

Savings/Retirement Plan $_____

Total $_____

Monthly Savings Goal:

$_____

Monthly Budget Sacrifice Item:

_____

Month_____

Monthly Plan of Action to Recondition My Mindset

_____

_____

_____

_____

_____

_____

_____

_____

Income

Salary (1) $_____ Salary (2) $_____

Cash $_____

Child Support/Alimony $_____

Investment Income $_____

Other Income Resources $_____

Total $_____

Expenses

Rent/Mortgage $_____

Homeowners/Rental Insurance $_____

Utilities $_____

Internet/Cable/Telephone $_____

Transportation/Car Payment $_____

Child Care $_____

Insurance (Car) $_____

Insurance (Life/Disability/Medical) $_____

Groceries/Dining $_____

Clothing $_____

Entertainment $_____

Travel (Business/Personal) $_____

Education/Training $_____

Grooming (Hair/Nails) $_____

Savings/Retirement Plan $_____

Total $_____

Monthly Savings Goal:

$_____

Monthly Budget Sacrifice Item:

_____

Month_____

Monthly Plan of Action to Recondition My Mindset

_____

_____

_____

_____

_____

_____

_____

Income

Salary (1) $_____ Salary (2) $_____

Cash $_____

Child Support/Alimony $_____

Investment Income $_____

Other Income Resources $_____

Total $_____

Expenses

Rent/Mortgage $_____

Homeowners/Rental Insurance $_____

Utilities $_____

Internet/Cable/Telephone $_____

Transportation/Car Payment $_____

Child Care $_____

Insurance (Car) $_____

Insurance (Life/Disability/Medical) $_____

Groceries/Dining $_____

Clothing $_____

Entertainment $_____

Travel (Business/Personal) $_____

Education/Training $_____

Grooming (Hair/Nails) $_____

Savings/Retirement Plan $_____

Total $_____

N OTES:

S H Y N N A M I T C H E L L

The Financial Fanatic Financial & Business Empowerment Coach/Author /Speaker/Realtor

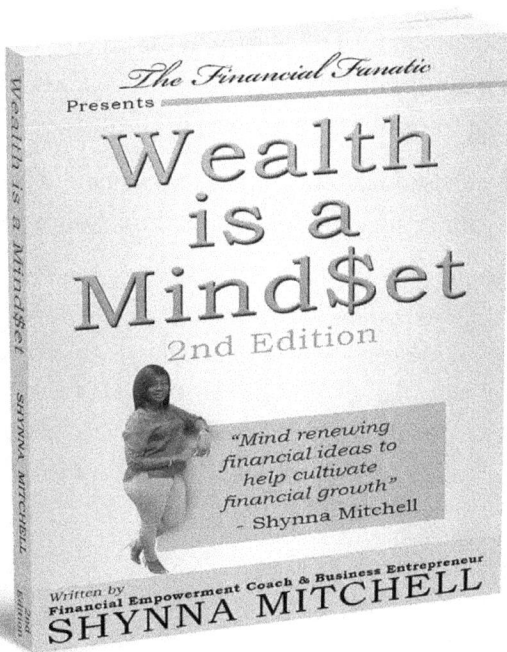

Empowering you to build your empire...

"Wealth is a Mind$et!" SHYNNA MITCHELL says these days—as she pens this empowering resource journal about "keeping it real" with your current financial position, identifying challenges, and taking responsibility for changing the way you view wealth.

In a world of economic ups & downs, we must begin by examining financial culture and what we have been taught as it relates to money and wealth. Though finances are a very private area for most to discuss, it is a crucial topic that will help us to understand the root of our financial 'woes' as well as the fruit of our financial 'favor'; which is essential to our overall growth of wealth.

—We must educate ourselves and organically retrain our brains about how we think about wealth.

"One of my goals for writing this book was for it to be used as a resource tool of empowerment. I wanted to share my experience as well as the positive and mind-renewing financial ideas that I used in my journey to help my reading audience to also recondition their mindsets."—SHYNNA MITCHELL

Available on Amazon & Other Retail Outlets

Wealth is a Mind$et 2nd Edition by SHYNNA MITCHELL

When purchasing books for class attendees, group sessions or gifts bulk rates and discounts may be made available.

SHYNNA MITCHELL The Financial Fanatic Financial & Business Empowerment Coach/Author /Speaker/Realtor

Email: info@wealthisamindset.org

Website: Wealthisamindset.org

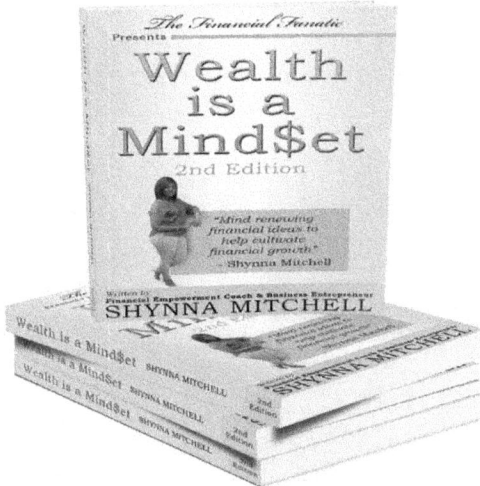

www.ingramcontent.com/pod-product-compliance
Lightning Source LLC
Chambersburg PA
CBHW070036100426
42740CB00013B/2706